COPING WITH
Compulsive
Eating

Carolyn Simpson

ROSEN PUBLISHING GROUP, INC./NEW YORK

Published in 1997 by The Rosen Publishing Group, Inc.
29 East 21st Street, New York, NY 10010

First Edition

Library of Congress Cataloging-in-Publication Data
Simpson, Carolyn.
    Coping with compulsive eating / Carolyn Simpson.
        p.   cm. — (Coping)
    Includes bibliographical references and index.
    Summary: Discusses types of compulsive eating, the physical and
    social consequences of this behavior, and solutions that do not
    include dieting but address physical or emotional problems and
    unhealthy patterns of behavior.
        ISBN 0-8239-2516-1
    1. Compulsive eating—Juvenile literature.   [1. Compulsive
    eating.   2. Eating disorders.]   I. Title.   II. Series.
    RC552.C65S475   1997
    616.85′26—dc21   97-20478
                                                                              CIP
                                                                               AC

Manufactured in the United States of America

ABOUT THE AUTHOR ◇

Carolyn Simpson is an outpatient therapist at Family Mental Health Center, a division of Parkside, Inc., in Tulsa, Oklahoma. In addition, she teaches psychology and human relations courses at Tulsa Community College. She has worked with numerous clients who have compulsive disorders, including compulsive eating. Over the years she has worked as a clinical social worker, a school counselor, a teacher, and a writer. This is her nineteenth book. Others include *Coping with Emotional Disorders* and *Careers in Social Work* (both coauthored with her husband), *Coping with an Unplanned Pregnancy*, and *Coping Through Conflict Resolution and Peer Mediation*.

Mrs. Simpson lives with her husband and their three children on the outskirts of Tulsa.

Contents

Introduction

If we ate only when we were hungry (and then took in only as much as our bodies needed), there would be no reason for this book.

Eating is both social and psychological; it does a lot more for us than just keep our bodies nourished. Most people experience this firsthand—rummaging through the cupboards after a bad day at school, or eating cookies "just because they're there." You may be surprised to find how many different reasons people give for eating. See if you can recognize yourself in any of these settings:

We eat as a form of socializing. If people want to be together, going out to eat is just "something to do." This could happen on a date or in a group. Diners and cafés are places where you can hang out and talk without being around parents or teachers, and usually you can stay (and eat) for as long as you like.

Also, people go to parties and stand around the tables of food. Some take a plate, pile on the food, and start nibbling. Eating gives them something to do so they feel less conspicuous standing around.

We also eat to be polite. Has a friend ever offered you some cake or brownies she'd just baked? You didn't want to offend her, so you took three pieces and ate them all even though you weren't hungry for the first one.

We eat in reaction to emotional needs. You may eat

when you're bored or lonely simply because you associate food with love and comfort. When you were a baby, you were given a bottle when you cried. When you got older and skinned a knee, you may have been given cookies to make you feel better. This may explain why many people look to food to comfort or distract them when they hurt.

You may eat when you're angry, and that has nothing to do with hunger, either. Food is believed to make you feel calmer, but it's not a substitute for handling anger more constructively.

You may eat when you're happy. You may have just won a big basketball game, so you go out to celebrate. Food, in this case, is a reward.

We eat because it's a habit. Not all people are hungry at lunchtime, but most go ahead and eat anyway. Why? Because it's lunchtime, and you're supposed to eat at lunchtime. You may have eaten a midmorning snack, but because of your upbringing, feel compelled to eat at noon anyway.

Many people associate food with certain activities. When you go to the movies, you may buy popcorn because you always eat popcorn when you go to the movies. Some people reach for something to nibble on when they talk on the phone. Others always sample the food they're preparing, not because they're hungry, but because that's the way they cook. They eat because they are in situations in which they're accustomed to having food.

We eat when we see something tasty or smell something delicious. You may not be hungry to start with, but you pass a bakery and catch the aroma. Unable to put the food out of your mind, you go back, buy something, and eat it because it smells so good.

We eat because food is available. You may not be able to resist opening the box of Oreos just because it's there in the cupboard. Or you help yourself to a handful of freshly baked cookies because they're cooling on the counter. In neither case were you eating because you were hungry; the food was there, and you reacted.

The five settings described above have little to do with the physical need for food, but more with how people think about food. Food is a habit, or it is a means to achieve relief, comfort, or happiness.

This behavior is usually normal, and can come and go. For example, you may eat a whole bag of gummy bears each day the week before you take your driver's test, but stop when the test is behind you. Or someone at work talks about how much he loves barbecue-flavored potato chips, and you can't help but make a detour to the snack aisle at the grocery store on the way home.

But you may also find that eating has become more than just a whim. You either can't stop thinking about food— what you're going to eat, and when—or you can't stop eating after you start. Instead of fading as time passes, your preoccupation with food grows more intense. You don't think about much else.

Perhaps you live in a family in which every night at dinner, food is heaped on your plate, and you're expected to eat all of it. Even though this leaves you unpleasantly full, you find that even when you're not at home, you're always stuffing yourself at meals.

You may hide food, and eat in private. Or you feel fat after eating, so you start a habit of throwing up. Or you see yourself becoming very overweight. These are all unhealthy behaviors, and they're what this book is about. You may be a compulsive eater.

As you read further, you will see that there are different types of compulsive eaters, and different reasons why people become compulsive eaters. There are also different remedies. This book was written to help you recognize the signs of compulsive eating, and to point you in the right direction for seeking help.

PART ◇ I

WHAT IS COMPULSIVE EATING?

CHAPTER 1

Types of Compulsive Eating

Compulsive eating, like other types of compulsive behavior, involves doing things that you realize are harmful but you can't stop. You find yourself thinking about food all the time: either how to get it or how to avoid it. *Because you are unable to control yourself around certain foods, you are a compulsive eater.*

Let's look at the different types of behaviors that constitute compulsive eating.

BINGEING AND PURGING

Sharon's English teacher was handing back exams. Sharon knew she hadn't done well. When the teacher looked at the floor as she handed Sharon her exam, Sharon knew it was bad. Her stomach started to churn.

Sharon stole a quick glance at the red numbers in the upper right corner. **66.**

"66. What's a 66?" Sharon thought wildly. "Is that just a C, or is it a D? Does it even matter? It isn't an A. What will my parents say?" Her thoughts kept crashing into each other.

Sharon hid her paper in her notebook. She was feeling weak, and all she could think about was food. She was supposed to go over to her friend Jana's after school and work on their project for Spanish, but she knew she wouldn't do that. Maybe later she could think about the project. Right now, all she could think about was eating cookie dough ice cream.

All through her last class, she debated buying that carton of ice cream.

"I shouldn't eat it," she told herself. "I'll regret it.

"Maybe I'll just buy it and hide it in the freezer. If I still want it later, then I'll eat some.

"Who are you kidding?" she thought. "If you buy it, you'll eat it. And that'll just be the beginning."

Sharon had almost made up her mind not to buy the ice cream when someone asked her what she'd gotten on the English exam. That settled it. She needed the ice cream.

Sharon skipped out on the project that afternoon and went alone to the grocery store. She grabbed a shopping basket and headed directly toward the freezer section. On the way, she spotted a guy from her English class.

"I can't let him see me buying ice cream," she thought. So she headed to the salad bar and made herself a large vegetable and lettuce salad instead. Then she bought a box of crackers to go with the salad. But she still wasn't ready to head for the checkout line. She kept thinking about that half gallon of ice cream.

"I could always tell that guy my parents were having a party and needed this stuff," she told herself.

She turned back toward the freezer section. On the way she passed the cookie aisle and piled a few packages of cookies into the basket. Then she found her ice cream, placing a carton of cookie dough and a carton of caramel fudge (because she couldn't decide between the two) into her basket. At last she made her way to the checkout.

Once she had paid for the food, she hurried out to the car. As soon as she got home, she piled all the food on the counter. Her mother would be home in an hour and a half, so she had to eat fast.

She started with the salad. The salad could have fed three people, but Sharon ate it all herself. Then she ate the whole box of crackers. She scooped out half the carton of cookie dough ice cream and half the caramel fudge into a serving dish. She ate the ice cream, then moved on to the cookies. At first she felt dreamy and contented as she ate, but then her stomach started to feel as if it would burst. Sharon looked at the clock. Her mother would be home in forty minutes. She couldn't leave any evidence. She had to eat everything. Besides, she couldn't leave any of it unfinished. No matter how stuffed, she had to finish it all.

At last, she'd downed the ice cream, cookies, crackers, and salad. She threw the empty cartons in the trash, tied up the trash bag, and brought it to the trash can. Then, she put a new liner in the kitchen waste basket and headed for the bathroom.

She was feeling horrible. She started to run some bath water; her mother wouldn't wonder why Sharon was in the tub when she got home from work. That's often where she was this time of day.

She lifted the toilet lid, stuck her fingers down her throat and vomited up all the food she had just eaten so desperately. It took a few times before she was satisfied all the food was gone.

Exhausted, she took off her clothes and climbed into the tub to soak and rest. She was too tired to feel the anxiety she'd felt earlier about her low grade. Besides, all she could feel now was the guilt from spending money and wasting all that food. She hadn't really enjoyed any of it, and worse, she hadn't been able to control herself at all. She hated herself when she did this.

"I won't do this ever again," she told herself. "In fact, I'll skip dinner."

Laura had been hospitalized a week now for compulsively starving herself. She knew that the whole staff monitored what she ate, and she lost privileges if she didn't eat. They even escorted her to the bathroom so she wouldn't throw up the food afterward. As a result, Laura was feeling fat and out of control.

She'd tried increasing her exercise routine, but the nurses had caught on to her nighttime exercising and monitored that activity too. It seemed as if everyone was conspiring to make her fat.

However, Laura had another way of getting rid of food. Throughout the day, she made calls to different relatives and friends, telling them she was constipated and asking them to bring her some Ex-Lax. Not considering the laxative a medication, her friends and family complied. Some visited that day; some visited the next day; and some visited during the evenings. Laura collected boxes and boxes of laxatives. Then, when forced to eat a regular meal, Laura used the laxatives to get rid of it.

"They can't blame me for getting diarrhea, can they?" she thought.

Only, Laura didn't take one or two tablets. She knew that wouldn't work because she'd tried it often in the past. Laura needed twenty or thirty laxatives at a time to bring about the relief she wanted. When she managed to get a town pass to go home for a few hours, she dropped by the drugstore and purchased all the laxatives available. After a month in the hospital, she was sneaking eighty laxatives a day.

Under normal circumstances, people get hungry at regular intervals throughout the day, eat when they're hungry, and don't think much about food until they're hungry again. They eat what they need and stop when they're satisfied. They don't plan their days around what they'll eat or what they won't eat.

If you are a compulsive eater, it's different. You may think about food all day long—either about what you're going to eat next, or about what you won't let yourself eat. Compulsive eaters may seem to be very controlled—often they're on diets—but privately, they always feel "out of control."

People who binge and purge have a disorder called bulimia. Bulimics are considered compulsive overeaters who force themselves to get rid of the food afterward. Some people induce vomiting, like Sharon. Others, like Laura, who either can't get away with vomiting or don't want to throw up, use laxatives to force a bout with diarrhea. Most people don't know, though, that once the food makes it to the intestines, most of the calories are already absorbed.

An eating binge is defined as an abnormally large

amount of food eaten at one sitting. That could include whole cartons of ice cream, boxes of cookies, whole roasted chickens, liters of soda, and whole loaves of bread. In an eating binge, a person can consume more than 10,000 calories in one sitting. Then, the very thought of having eaten all those calories scares her into purging.

Some purgers have eaten and vomited so often (up to ten times a day) that they only have to walk to the bathroom and decide to vomit for the reflex to happen. Some people have to retrain their bodies once they stop purging because it has become a habit to vomit after eating.

Despite this behavior, most other people never suspect that someone is bingeing and purging. In general, a person who binges and purges isn't thin or emaciated, but isn't overweight either. If she's purging, she usually manages to keep the weight off, even when taking in large quantities of food. So, you can look at an average size person and never suspect that she throws up every meal she eats.

Additionally, people who binge and purge do so privately. In public, they may look like normal eaters. They may even stay away from food altogether. But the anxiety generated from such rigid control and deprivation may lead to another eating binge later.

COMPULSIVE OVEREATING

Jack was looking forward to the holidays—not so much for the presents, but for the food his mother liked to cook for the relatives. And then there was the caramel cheesecake his Aunt Marilyn always brought, Cousin Martha's white chocolate fudge, and Stacy's glazed candied yams with marshmallows.

Jack had been to plenty of Christmas parties at the

homes of his friends this year, but he could never eat comfortably when his friends were hanging around. He sometimes tried to stay away from the tables of food because he would be more interested in the finger sandwiches, cheese trays, and desserts than he would be in the people at the party. Better that he not eat at all.

With his relatives, it was different. They all had big appetites and knew how to enjoy a good meal. In fact, that's where Jack learned to love food. Both his parents were overweight, as were most of his aunts and uncles. Whenever they cooked a meal, they would urge everyone to eat two and sometimes three helpings of everything.

Holidays were opportunities to celebrate, and his family always celebrated with food. Food, celebrating, and love were all wrapped up together. The only problem was that Jack hated the way he lost control around food.

This holiday was no different. Jack ate three helpings of everything. He started to feel stuffed, but he didn't want to miss anything.

Later, Jack joined his cousins on a walk around the neighborhood. Upon his return, he headed for the kitchen to nibble some more. He cut himself another slice of cheesecake and settled down on the couch to enjoy it.

Sixty to seventy million people are compulsive overeaters. Of that number, 85 percent are women. Not all of them binge by eating huge amounts at a sitting. Some people simply eat small amounts of food all day long.

Unlike the people you read about earlier in this chapter, overeaters do not purge afterward. If they overeat and don't fast or diet, they ultimately become overweight. Some 22 percent of children in the United States are obese (weigh 30 percent more than their ideal body weight). But people's eating behavior can vary greatly.

For example, some people eat fast and furiously. As you'll see later, this behavior is usually learned from watching others. After a while, they become accustomed to the overstuffed feeling and associate that with any meal.

Some compulsive overeaters nibble instead of binge. They spread their eating out over the day or night. They will never eat a whole box of cookies or a family-size bag of chips in one sitting, but will eat both over the space of a few hours.

Sometimes compulsive eating starts with dieting. This can start the cycle of starving and bingeing. People stick to a rigid diet all day long, particularly when they're around other people, and eat late at night or when they're alone. Then, they binge on all the food they denied themselves during the days or week past.

Some compulsive eaters started out as plate-cleaners. They are simply obedient children who learned at an early age to eat everything on their plates. So, whether or not they ever learned to realize when they were full, they couldn't act on the realization. They had to keep eating, even when their stomachs told them "No more!" After a while, many plate-cleaners simply eat everything in front of them without asking themselves whether they're hungry or stuffed.

Finally, some compulsive eaters are comfort-eaters. They eat normal amounts of food most of the time, except when they're stressed. Then they turn to food to make themselves feel better, either by bingeing or perpetually nibbling.

Most compulsive eaters either wage a constant war with their weight by dieting or they become overweight. Even if they've managed to maintain a relatively average weight, they know they have an unhealthy relationship with food. People who are overweight also face the pressure from a society that is obsessed with thinness.

In the next chapter, I'll talk about these and other consequences of compulsive eating.

CHAPTER 2

The Physical and Social Consequences of Eating Problems

Compulsive eating has many effects on your well-being. First, I'll talk about the physical problems that can occur if you eat compulsively. There are many consequences for your social life and self-image, too.

PHYSICAL EFFECTS OF BINGEING AND PURGING

The cycle of bingeing and purging has many medical consequences. People who purge by vomiting may find themselves vomiting after *every* meal, whether they want to or not. After months of vomiting several times a day, the body reflexively vomits after anything goes down the throat. This acquired response to food leads to malnutrition.

Excessive vomiting also causes other problems. Bringing up stomach contents is a forceful job, and can damage the stomach. Add to that the fact that stomach contents are very acidic (acid in the stomach helps digest the food), and you run the risk of damaging the esophagus. People who throw up a lot may get a "chipmunk" look, because their cheeks swell. Stomach acid also erodes the enamel on their teeth. In severe cases, the throat bleeds.

Whether people purge by vomiting or using laxatives, the biggest risk is dehydration. When it's dehydrated, the body has lost fluids, and important minerals have been washed out along with the fluids. Skin dries out and loses its elasticity; hair loses its shine. The contents of the digestive tract dry out as well, which causes constipation.

Dehydration also leads to a mineral imbalance in the body, which causes bloating, abdominal pain, and gas. While bloating and abdominal pain will make you feel uncomfortable, continued dehydration could lead to kidney failure and cardiac arrest.

Long-term laxative use has the opposite effect on the body from excessive vomiting. Excessive vomiting causes a reflexive reaction; a person vomits more easily after practice. Using a lot of laxatives causes the colon to lose its ability to move on its own; it becomes dependent upon the laxatives. Unfortunately, the quantity of laxatives required increases over time, which leads to dehydration and potassium loss.

SPECIFIC EFFECTS OF SUGAR ABUSE

Sugar abuse is another consequence of eating compulsively.

When people eat nutritious food, the nutrients are changed into glucose, which the body uses for fuel. The pancreas releases insulin to help process the glucose in the bloodstream and get it into the cells and muscles. When you eat foods high in sugar, you get a quick jolt of sugar right into the bloodstream. All that sugar triggers the pancreas to produce a larger amount of insulin than normal. The insulin quickly takes care of the sugar, but the blood glucose level drops just as quickly. This is called crave/crash syndrome. People binge on sugar, and then feel awful once the greater amount of insulin has processed the sugar out of the bloodstream. Then they want more sugar.

Sugar abuse may contribute to two dangerous conditions: hypoglycemia and diabetes.

Hypoglycemia results when blood levels of glucose drop too low to fuel the body's activity. If you eat a lot of sugar and then vomit, you may show symptoms similar to those of hypoglycemia. Your body produces more insulin to take care of large amount of sugar you ate. But after you vomit, your body still holds the excessive insulin, and it doesn't have any sugar to process. You may feel shaky, dizzy, cold, and clammy. You also may experience anxiety or rapid mood changes. Other conditions can contribute to hypoglycemia as well: early pregnancy, prolonged fasting, long periods of strenuous exercise, taking beta blocker medications, or chronic or binge drinking. It is important to see your doctor if you experience symptoms of hypoglycemia, so the underlying cause can be found.

Hypoglycemia also is a complication of diabetes. Diabetes is a condition in which the body can't use glucose for fuel: either the pancreas isn't able to make enough insulin, or the insulin that is available isn't effective. While diets high in sugars are not believed to cause diabetes, other behavior can cause symptoms of hypo-glycemia in diabetics, including taking too much medica-tion or missing or delaying a meal.

Diabetes is a permanent condition as well. If not prop-erly treated, a diabetic faces complications with all his other medical conditions. If he gets too much insulin, he can go into insulin shock and die. Before he gets to that point, though, he may look and act oddly. He may get combative and not recognize his loved ones. If he has too much sugar (and isn't given insulin), he can fall into a coma and die.

Sugar abuse leads to other problems. You probably already know that too much sugar leads to tooth decay, even if you brush your teeth three times a day. But most people don't know that too much sugar can lead to a calcium deficiency. The body needs calcium for strong bones, but sugar imbalances lead to too much calcium getting deposited in the form of kidney stones.

Most people recognize that the extremes of overeating and starving one's self lead to serious medical problems. However, one is less inclined to see the dangers in binge-ing when it's accompanied by purging. Adolescents seem to think that as long as you quickly get rid of the food you've eaten, your body won't be harmed. The truth is that you can never get rid of food before at least some of it gets into the bloodstream. Purging is a great danger to the body.

PHYSICAL CONSEQUENCES OF OVEREATING (WITHOUT PURGING)

Compulsively overeating leads to several serious medical problems. One of the common results of overeating is obesity, which puts a tremendous strain on the heart and complicates all other medical problems. Someone who eats a lot of high-fat foods is likely to end up with high blood pressure, which is a major cause of strokes. Also, eating a lot of sugary foods doesn't give someone as much nutrition as do whole foods such as fruits, vegetables, and grains.

Overweight people also are more prone to injury because they weigh more than their bodies can adequately support. Being overweight contributes to or exaggerates back problems and can cause respiratory problems. Whenever overweight people have surgery, they're at greater risk. They also are candidates for sleep apnea, a life-threatening condition in which excess skin in someone's throat interferes with breathing when he falls asleep at night. When this person lies on his back, either his tongue or the excess skin falls into the back of his throat, obstructing the airway, and he stops breathing. After several seconds, the oxygen level in his blood drops, and the person gulps in a fresh supply of air, waking himself in the process. This scenario replays itself as often as 300 times a night, preventing the person from getting a full night's sleep.

Obesity is also connected to fertility problems. If an extremely overweight woman gets pregnant, the pregnancy is considered high risk. She'll have to be monitored closely to make sure both she and the baby do well.

SOCIAL CONSEQUENCES OF COMPULSIVE EATING

Whether or not you're overweight, if you are a compulsive eater, you probably are very uncomfortable around food in public. You may try to avoid occasions and places where food will be. That takes you out of the mainstream. Parties, banquets, dinners, and proms are all equally difficult because they involve food. When you do go out, you may decline to eat anything. Also, compulsively watching and controlling your behavior around food can eventually lead to binge eating later on.

Compulsive eating also is influenced by societal values. American society places a premium on attractiveness, and part of being attractive is being thin—even thinner than is healthy or normal. Therefore, people who are overweight (especially if they're obese) are not considered attractive or appealing. Because society generally deems them undesirable, they are often ostracised.

People who are significantly overweight have trouble getting picked for school teams, getting hired over their slimmer peers, or being "teacher's pets." Of course, it is discriminatory, but unfortunately it's the way some people behave in our society. Just as people are prejudiced against certain races, the elderly, and adolescents, many are prejudiced against the overweight. Many overweight teens are the butts of cruel jokes played by unsympathetic classmates. This treatment has lasting consequences for someone's self-image and self-esteem. It also plays a part in developing, or maintaining, an eating disorder.

However, compulsive eating, and bingeing and purging, often have less to do with concern over your weight than with underlying emotional needs. Society's pressures and ideals of thinness certainly are important contributors to the problem. At this point you need to look inward, and examine all of the important circumstances surrounding your feelings about food and eating. This is the subject of the next part of the book.

CAUSES OF COMPULSIVE EATING

CHAPTER 3

Is It Biological?

I t's difficult to say how many people are compulsive eaters due to biological factors. Nutritionists and doctors may be more prone to blame biological events than psychologists and psychiatrists are. Compulsive eaters themselves may prefer to believe they act from physiological reasons because these explanations don't involve emotions. For many people, it's easier to take mineral supplements and prescription medications than it is to examine their feelings, which is the subject of the next chapter.

Most compulsive eaters, however, suffer from a combination of biological and psychological factors. Even if a cause of an eating disorder is psychological, poor nutrition can alter your thinking process. If you compulsively overeat, strong sugar fluctuations and mineral imbalances may lead to cravings.

Nutritional explanations for compulsive eating hold that people compulsively eat certain foods when their bodies are lacking key minerals. One example is if your diet is too high in calcium and too low in magnesium. We absorb calcium only when we take in more magnesium than calcium, so if the minerals are not in balance, we will be deficient in magnesium and the excess calcium becomes toxic. Imbalances in minerals can lead to binges.

SUGAR CRAVINGS

If you're hypoglycemic, you may turn to sugar to ease the physical symptoms of low blood sugar. People with hypoglycemia have too little glucose, or fuel, in their bloodstreams. Consequently, they get the "shakes," and may feel weak, dizzy, and sometimes depressed. While eating complex carbohydrates would keep them on an even keel longer, it wouldn't correct their symptoms very quickly. Sugar provides the quick fix. When people eat sugar, the bloodstream gets a jolt of glucose. However, the pancreas has to secrete a larger amount of insulin than normal to process this sugar, and so the sugar is quickly used up.

Eating sugar, then, causes a rebound effect. Once you start eating it, you have to keep eating it because the symptoms of low blood sugar return so quickly. With hypoglycemia, your body has an abnormal glucose metabolism, and you process sugar, as well as other foods, more quickly than normal. The efforts to keep low blood sugar at bay result in compulsive eating.

Hypoglycemia and sugar cravings can also result from insufficient amounts of chromium in your body. Chromium is a trace mineral that helps transport glucose into cell tissue. When chromium is in short supply, your body can become insulin-resistant. Even though your pancreas secretes sufficient insulin, without chromium the cells won't necessarily pick up the insulin, and it will be excreted from the body. An imbalance in the glucose metabolism, stemming from the shortage of chromium, will cause both hypoglycemic symptoms and sugar cravings.

Sugar cravings also can stem from a condition called candida, which is a yeast infection. Sugar feeds this yeast infection, so people with untreated yeast infections often crave huge amounts of sugar. Everyone harbors the organism *Candida albicans* in his or her body. If a person's body is in balance, the *candida* doesn't become a problem. However, factors such as hormonal changes, diets rich in sugar, and long-term antibiotic use can upset the chemical balance and can cause the fungus *candida* to overrun the body. Compulsively eating sugary foods may trigger the *candida* overgrowth, as well as sustain it.

FOOD SENSITIVITIES AND ALLERGIES

People don't often think of sensitivities as causing us to eat more of a substance that can hurt us, but that's exactly what happens. Ordinarily allergies cause hives, headaches, or bronchial spasms. Then people clearly know they should avoid certain foods or products.

However, food sensitivities don't always cause such clear-cut reactions. If you have a food sensitivity, your body probably is not able to completely digest the food's proteins. When the proteins are not digested, the undigested molecules reach the tissues through the bloodstream. These undigested protein molecules look like foreign matter, and so your body produces antibodies to defend against them. The next time you eat this food, your immune system will attack the partially digested protein molecules as invaders. This is the allergic reaction; but instead of getting hives, you start craving huge amounts of the very foods your body can't handle. Sugar and white flour are common problematic foods.

While eating foods you're allergic to, you're more likely to catch viruses—your immune system is weakened in order to handle the food. People with food sensitivities often get headaches and feel tired without understanding that it's a result of a particular food they've eaten. Then, ironically, they start compulsively eating the offending food.

FOOD ADDICTIONS

Many people believe that we can become addicted to certain foods, especially highly refined carbohydrates, chocolate, and caffeine. An addict is a person who continues to use a substance compulsively without caring about the negative consequences. He knows that what he is doing is harmful, but he continues to do it anyway. Food addiction is similar to alcohol and drug addiction in that it occurs in stages.

Stage 1 involves the person's preoccupation with the addiction. Whether a person has a food sensitivity or seeks food for comfort, she thinks about food most of the day. She may plan menus, cook meals for her family, or calculate how many calories she can safely handle that day. She may keep food in her room, and eat when she's alone.

Stage II of the addiction occurs when the person has a hard time limiting the amount of food he consumes. The food addict may try to maneuver himself so that others do not suspect his addiction. For example, if he buys a large quantity of food at the grocery store, he may tell people he's planning a party, although he may plan to eat the food himself.

By this point, the food addict is experiencing the consequences of overeating. He's very likely overweight (unless he's purging). He's probably tired a lot and unhappy with himself.

This leads to stage III, the final stage of addiction: a loss of interest in anything other than food. The food addict may decline going out, and withdraw into himself. This isolation most likely reinforces his compulsive eating.

Some people think it's too drastic to consider a compulsive overeater to be an addict. They reason that the overeater is simply not reining in his appetite. The people who subscribe to the theory of addiction say the compulsive overeater *can't* rein in his appetite: like other addictions, food addiction has a physical basis, and must be treated as such.

CHEMICAL IMBALANCES

The main brain chemicals that have to do with mood, pleasure, pain, and eating disorders are serotonin, dopamine, norepinephrine, and endorphins. When endorphins (the body's natural pain relievers) are in low supply, the brain is "on edge." People may turn to mood-altering substances to soothe the brain artificially. Often, that means using alcohol and drugs, but some people choose food. Chocolate, sugar, and caffeine all contain substances that alter levels of certain brain chemicals.

One of those chemicals, serotonin, is often called "the calming chemical." When you have a sufficient amount of serotonin in your brain, you are not as likely to be depressed, you sleep better, and you have more control over compulsive eating as well as other compulsive behavior.

Norepinephrine is another chemical closely linked with both mood and appetite. Sufficient amounts of norepinephrine signal the brain that you're hungry. Serotonin, in turn, tells the brain that you're full and can stop eating. Scientists have discovered that people who binge and purge have an unusually low level of serotonin. It's possible that they're not receiving messages from their brains that they're full, so they continue to overeat.

People with other types of compulsive behavior (like those common to obsessive compulsive disorder—washing their hands many times a day, checking to see if doors are locked, hoarding trash to excess) appear to respond to medications that raise the serotonin levels in the brain. With improved levels of this chemical, people seem better able to deal with their compulsions.

Because serotonin levels are important in helping us feel calm and in control, it's not surprising that people feel better when taking medications, such as Prozac, Zoloft, and Paxil, that increase serotonin levels. However, the carbohydrates in foods you crave can also increase your serotonin level.

Hormone levels can be responsible for compulsive eating as well. As you will see later in the book, the function of certain glands can greatly influence your eating patterns.

DIETING AND OVEREATING

Alan waged a constant battle with his weight. He ate a lot of sugar, so he started drinking diet colas and skipping desserts, but it didn't seem to affect his weight. He didn't realize that caffeinated drinks can set off sugar cravings just as easily as sugar-sweetened drinks can. Finally, he decided he couldn't manage his weight by dieting unless he was either very strict or simply went on a fast.

He tried a rigid diet first. The first week went pretty well; as long as he didn't eat anything not on the diet, he didn't crave the forbidden foods. Of course, he made excuses not to eat lunch with his friends because he couldn't eat his salads without wanting their french fries. By the second week, he was feeling deprived and finally gave in to the urge to eat "just one little french fry." He ultimately ate much more than a regular meal, since he was so starved.

"Diets don't work for me," he thought. "When I sit around other people, I want what they're eating. If I eat just one thing, I start craving a whole pile of food. Maybe I should fast."

Fasting allowed Alan to feel good about skipping meals. After all, he reasoned, he was purifying his system. On the days he didn't fast, he reasoned that he could eat anything he wanted. He tried fasting one day a week, but he quickly began to dread Tuesdays, the day he'd chosen to fast. The more he tried not to think about food, the more he thought about it.

The fast ended one night when he stayed up late studying. He'd gone the whole day depriving himself and was undernourished. By 10:00 pm he was raiding the refrigerator, consoling himself that he'd fasted all day. It was always following a fast that Alan overate the most.

There's a logical reason for overeating after a fast. Dieting sets us up for low blood sugar and extreme hunger. Feeling weak and dizzy makes us want to do whatever it takes to remedy the situation. We need a quick fix, and sugar is the best choice for raising blood-sugar levels quickly. Unfortunately, that activates the rebound effect, and we have to spend the next hour or two pumping ourselves full of sugar.

Extreme hunger, the result of fasting, leads us to binge

eating. We're simply so hungry that we don't pay any attention to how much we're taking in. Hurried eating leads to eating more than our bodies need.

These are the most common biological explanations for compulsive eating. As you'll see in later chapters, there are specific ways to treat them. However, there are emotional reasons for compulsive eating as well, which I will turn to now.

Emotional Reasons for Compulsive Eating

J oey Perez was the younger of two brothers. He was also the heavier of the two boys and seemed to be the one with all the bad luck. Both brothers were on the school football team, but while his brother, Lucas, was the gifted wide receiver, Joey was a second-string lineman who only played when their team was leading by twenty-four points.

Lucas was planning to go to college on a football scholarship; Joey had neither the grades nor the athletic skill to win a scholarship. That made him angry a lot of the time.

Whenever Lucas had an exceptionally good day on the field, Joey found himself at the neighborhood deli after the game. He ordered sandwiches, cole slaw, potato salad, and baked beans, and ate everything in silence. Sometimes he sat with his second-string teammates.

"Hey, man," a teammate would say, "Are you really going to eat all that?"

"Sure," Joey would say, hesitating with the fork to his mouth. "I didn't eat much for breakfast."

"Well, Lucas must have eaten his Wheaties. He sure had a good game, huh?"

"He always has a good game," Joey muttered, as he scooped up more potato salad. "Hey, are you going to finish that sandwich? I'll eat it if you're just going to let it go to waste."

Joey finished everything on his plate. He felt stuffed, as he always did after a game, but that was the whole point. Feeling stuffed, he went home and watched TV the rest of the night. What's more, he didn't have to feel that awful rage he felt when Lucas was once again the best man on the field.

EATING IN RESPONSE TO CONFLICT AND EMOTION

People eat for different reasons. Ideally, we should eat only because we are hungry and need *physical* nourishment. However, people also eat for *emotional* nourishment, or when certain feelings are uncomfortable.

Conflict is one common trigger of discomfort. Avoiding conflict can make you feel anxious, depressed, or angry. Moreover, any kind of conflict can lead to overeating. *Interpersonal* conflict flares up between two people or groups of people—for example, if you are fighting with your sister over who gets to use the car. *Intrapersonal* conflict, on the other hand, results from a conflict with your idealized self—in other words, what you think you *should* be. If you behave in ways that don't fit with your idealized picture of yourself—for example, if you act on the urge to hurt or insult someone—you feel guilt. Then, food becomes the means for you to distract and calm yourself.

Unfortunately, eating does not help to really deal with the conflict. Instead, people wind up feeling powerless, and may still turn to food.

Compulsive eaters turn to food to deal with this feeling, and others—anxiety, depression, boredom, anger, and fear. You may eat foods that you would ordinarily try to limit. What you like to overeat can depend on how you've feeling. If you are feeling unhappy or deprived, you may crave sweets; the more nurturance or reassurance you need, the more likely you'll turn to soft, creamy foods like ice cream or puddings. If you are angry, you may prefer snacks you have to crunch and chew hard, like nuts. If you are anxious, you may simply want to keep popping things in your mouth, like chips.

You may eat in response to happiness, too, because you think you don't deserve to be happy. Unconsciously, you may know that overeating brings pain and embarrassment. Eating compulsively when things are going well, then, reinforces low self-esteem.

NON-PHYSICAL HUNGER

Because eating is often a response to emotion, it's common for compulsive eaters to substitute physical hunger for emotional hunger. They are most likely looking for nurturance, either in relationships or from food.

Many people overcompensate for hunger they had in childhood. Home usually is where the food is, both figuratively and literally—but for others, home is where food was in short supply. Babies who went hungry despite their crying for food may grow up terrified of that gnawing feeling in their bellies. As young adults, they'll eat, not out of hunger, but to avoid *ever* being hungry.

COVERING UP ABUSE

Sometimes people turn to food to calm themselves after emotional, physical, or sexual abuse.

In cases like this, food serves more than one purpose. Food is comforting, but it also is a distancing device. Girls who are continually abused may unconsciously overeat to gain weight, believing that if they make themselves "unattractive" by society's standards, the abuse (especially if it's sexual) will stop. Some girls use this same tactic when trying to keep boyfriends at arms' length. If they're perceived as unattractive, maybe they won't be pushed into sexual activity they don't feel ready for.

Compulsive eating is also a way to punish yourself. Although it is comforting in the short-term, it makes people feel bad in the long-term. If people gain weight, they reason they've been bad and deserve to suffer the consequences.

Also, therapists have long suspected the link between bingeing and purging behavior and sexual abuse. Victims of sexual abuse may go on eating binges to numb their feelings of horror at what they've been through or are still enduring. The purging then serves a dual purpose—to get rid of the calories, and to get rid of the images of the abuse. The victim is vomiting up her "experience of ugliness." One of my patients once told me she felt better only when she'd made herself vomit. She would go through repeated cycles of bingeing and purging to wear herself out and obliterate the image of her abuser.

Many people who feel they have no control over their lives, especially if they're being abused, try to take control of their eating. It is important to address the bulimic's need to control her intake and stop purging, but it also is necessary to address the feelings that might be prompting her to eat compulsively.

EATING AS LEARNED BEHAVIOR

Children learn how to behave in great part by watching the adults around them. Children observe more of what people do than what people say, and they imitate what they see. For some children, that means learning unhealthy eating patterns.

For example, Roger came from a large family. Whenever the eight of them sat down at the dinner table, it turned into a war zone. Concerned about getting their share, both the kids and the adults overindulged. Knowing they wouldn't get another chance, they'd take two helpings of everything. George would lean over his sister's plate to grab some dinner rolls and stash a couple of extras in his lap. Gina would fill her plate with vegetables, salad, and chicken, even though she didn't like all the things she took. Even Roger's mother worried that her family wouldn't leave her much, so she sampled most of the meal beforehand. The family finished dinner in as quickly as ten minutes and then left the table in a daze. They never talked to each other except to say "Hand me the chicken" or "Send the green beans this way."

Not surprisingly, all of the kids had trouble eating at their friends' houses because they were never able to wait for people to pass them food.

Roger usually brought his lunch to school because it was hard for him to stand in line and wait while others chose their food. He would have had to fight down the urge to take the biggest pieces of turkey or the cookie with the most chocolate chips. "It's not that I'm even hungry for all that," Roger once explained to a counselor. "It's just that I feel if I don't get a pile of food when it's first offered, I'll never get another chance."

Roger learned to eat voraciously because everyone else in his family did. Anyone who ate his meal leisurely found the serving dishes empty before he got to sample any. People were in such a hurry to "get their fair share" that they never realized they were overeating at every meal. As a result, they learned to eat fast, barely chewing their food, and then associated that stuffed-to-the-gills feeling with every meal.

People who eat voraciously have usually learned this behavior. In some cases, children are merely copying the way their parents eat, even if current circumstances don't explain their hurried style. Parents brought up in poverty may eat more than they need to eat because of the desire to "never go hungry again." When they have children, their children watch how much or how fast their parents eat, and they learn it as the normal behavior. Thus, some children eat as if they're afraid of going hungry even when that isn't the case. They have merely learned to eat the way their parents eat.

It's a hard pattern to change, even once children leave home. Even though their parents won't follow them around to make sure they "eat everything on their plates," children internalize the value themselves and learn to disregard the signals that tell them they're full. If there is food still in front of them, it's meant to be eaten, especially if it's already been paid for.

Also, just as food can serve as a reward for doing well, it can serve as a consolation prize for losing. Some children learn to eat when they've lost because that's how their parents consoled them when they lost a race or didn't make a high grade as kids. Patterns of behavior are difficult to change, even when they're self-destructive patterns. Using food as a reward or a consolation prize sets children up to become "emotional eaters" later on.

Power Struggles

Many times food is not an end in itself but a means to an end. People have been known to use food and resulting weight gain as weapons against each other.

A neighbor who is a slim, attractive young woman has beautiful, but heavier, adolescent daughter. Millie has been fighting with her daughter for years. While they disagree about a lot of things, their fights always erupt over food. Millie prepares low-calorie meals because she worries about Rose's "weight problem," but Rose dislikes the low-calorie food and buys fast-food hamburgers to supplement her mother's meals. Rose also likes candy and sweets.

It's a constant battle. Millie threatens Rose, saying things like, "If you keep eating like this, I won't spend any more money on new clothes for you!" She occasionally bribes Rose, promising, "If you lose five pounds by the end of the month, I'll let you have a sleepover." Rose pretends to accommodate her mother, but she keeps eating as she pleases.

I asked Rose once how the diet was going, since Millie had announced to her neighbors that she and Rose were going on a new diet. Rose frowned. "I'm not on the diet anymore, but Mom's doing great. I think she's losing weight for both of us," she said.

"It's hard to be on a diet," I said.

"It is if you're like me and love food," Rose said.

"I guess that would make staying on a diet hard," I agreed.

"Well, I know Mom wants me to look like a model, but I don't care if I do. That's Mom's hangup. I'm okay the way I am."

I couldn't think of anything to say to that.

"Okay, so I know I'm overweight. It's all right with me. I just happen to love food. Let Mom be the model," Rose said.

It sounds as if Rose is genuinely happy with herself, and that the struggle is only her mother's problem. This may be partly true. But Rose also has learned that eating and gaining weight upsets her mother. She's learned that although she doesn't have a lot of control over some parts of her life, she can control what she eats and how she looks, which ultimately affects her mother. Rose is struggling to assert herself, and she's using food as one way to do it.

Eating as a Sign of Love

One of the lessons I learned growing up was that food is associated with love. If you really want to show someone you care about her, you make her a nice meal, or cook her favorite dessert, or take her out to dinner.

Early in my marriage, my husband complained that I rarely said "I love you."

"What do you mean?" I exclaimed. "I say it all the time. Don't you remember that lasagna I made you the other night? I made that from scratch. And what about the chocolate cheesecake? That took me hours to make."

"What's food got to do with love?" my husband asked.

"It shows I love you," I said, exasperated that he had to ask. "I made your favorite meal. Doesn't that tell you anything?"

"Well, how was I supposed to know what that meant?" he asked.

"Don't I always cook you your favorite desserts after a fight?" I asked.

"You mean you say you're sorry with food, too?" he asked.

"Of course," I said. "In my family, you say you're sorry with food, you say you're glad to see someone with food, you say you love someone by giving them food."

"It must be hard not to be overweight in your family," my husband said, smiling.

Eating Out of Habit

Many people eat compulsively when they're engaged in some activity. You may nibble while you talk on the phone; you may eat while you do your homework. You may overeat when you go to the movies. It is behavior learned at home. You may have noticed that Mom gathered some snacks together when she made a long-distance call to her old college roommate, or that Dad raided the refrigerator before every football game on television. You may have noticed your parents' willingness to buy you treats whenever you went to the movies. And because it was rewarding, you continued the behavior yourself, mostly out of habit.

When You Are Pressured to Eat

Some families use food as a way to manipulate each other. Everyone in Amy's family was overweight, except for Amy.

Amy was slender, and she didn't have to worry about what she ate. But her mother wasn't happy with her.

"Oh, Amy," she said. "Why don't you eat something. You're too skinny."

However, when Amy didn't gain weight, her mother started preparing her favorite desserts and leaving them around in plain sight. Amy found them hard to resist.

Amy started to gain weight. Then, feeling unhappy with herself, she'd stay home, which was just what her mother wanted. Amy's mother would say, "You're perfectly fine just the way you are."

Amy sometimes tried to break away from her family's grasp. She announced plans to attend a college out of state, but her mother soon became sick and asked her to pick a school closer to home in case she needed her.

When Amy started dating, her overweight sisters made fun of the guy Amy went out with and made fun of her for liking him. It soon became clear to Amy that her family seemed to like her only when she stayed home with them. It even occurred to her that they were encouraging her to overeat because they wanted her to feel "unwanted," the way they did. That way, Amy would never leave home.

While Amy resisted, her sisters clearly had learned that "the family that eats together, stays together."

The causes of compulsive eating are not always so clearly defined. Some people may be emotional eaters who learned at an early age to turn to food. Behavior that has been learned and reinforced in the family is hard to change because people have to change their attitudes as well as their habits. But once you learn to recognize the pressure, you can begin to manage compulsive eating. In the next chapters you will find specific ways to cure or cope.

WAYS TO CURE OR COPE

CHAPTER 5

Do Diets Work?

Patty thought she needed to lose weight because her compulsive eating had resulted in her being sixty pounds overweight. She didn't have the money to join a weight-loss program, and her parents couldn't afford to buy her the special food. So she decided to create her own diet, using liquid supplements and fasting.

Friends told her to fast first because it would rid her body of toxins and make it easier to stay on a diet. "After all, anything will taste great when all you've had is apple juice," one friend said.

So Patty spent the first day fasting. When she felt an overwhelming desire to eat something, she drank apple juice. She soon was sick of apple juice, and water didn't seem to taste as good after forcing herself to drink eight tall glasses a day.

However, Patty kept seeing pictures of herself as a slim model, and so she stuck to the fast. The next day she drank three chocolate malt diet drinks, and although they tasted better, she actually missed chewing food. By dinnertime, when she was supposed to eat a regular meal, she was so hungry for something to chew, she feared going overboard. So she substituted another liquid diet drink.

The next day she saw that she'd lost three pounds, and she was so elated that she decided to skip her third diet drink that day. For dinner that night, she ate potatoes and vegetables and a small piece of chicken. The next day, those three pounds had returned.

"I guess I have to be more strict with my regular meals," she told herself. That night she ate a couple of pieces of lettuce and some sugar-free Jello. Her parents had left early for a meeting and had no idea how poorly she was eating.

Patty found herself thinking more and more about food, and the more she thought about the things she was missing, the more she felt she had to punish herself. She ate less and less at each regular meal.

On the day she was supposed to give a speech in history, she stood up and fainted. Because her heartbeat was erratic, school nurses called an ambulance to take her to the hospital.

ANALYZING DIETS

Dieting is a big industry. The diet business is hard to ignore—it advertises on billboards, on television, and in the newspaper. Hundreds of products are on the market claiming to help people lose weight: over the counter diuretics (drugs that make your body excrete water); liquid meals; and appetite supressants that speed up your body's metabolism. Some companies create diet groups that model themselves after support groups. In these groups, the participants rally each other as they try to lose weight, and usually "weigh in" at certain intervals to check their "progress."

Some of these approaches to dieting are healthier than others. Belonging to a group of people who support each other is healthier than simply popping diet pills. But *all* diet products and organizations have two things in common:

- They are part of a business. And like any other business, they provide *services* in order to make a profit from *customers* (that's you).
- They encourage you to measure your success according to how much weight you lose.

There are big problems with the dieting model. First, since their business depends on the success of their products (and your subsequent weight loss), diet companies tend to emphasize strict regimens and short-term solutions. People are impatient: if you don't see a change in your weight, you will assume that the product doesn't work, and stop spending your money on it. Even the most forward-thinking diet groups encourage you to buy their brand of food, and attend their meetings. This is a lot of work. In fact, it's so much work, you most likely will get stressed out and quit—with good reason.

Second, the above pattern of short-term solutions, exasperation, and quitting only reinforces your thoughts about food. If you go off a diet, you may feel that you have "failed" somehow. This is an emotional issue. To make up for your bad feelings, you may try to restrict yourself in other ways. Patty, at the beginning of the chapter, followed this pattern. Binge eating also results from failed diets.

As a rule, *strict dieting only reinforces compulsive eating*.

Probably the biggest reason that diets aren't useful for compulsive eaters is because "losing weight" isn't the issue. As you know from reading earlier chapters, compulsive eating stems from a variety of causes and doesn't always result in weight gain. When you focus on losing a certain amount of weight, you lose sight of the bigger picture: the purpose food has been serving for you. Worse, people who are intent on losing weight, particularly within a certain time frame, may start on medically unsafe diets, as Patty did, with disastrous results.

Diets are not the answer to compulsive eating problems, but there are actual solutions. Realize that there are a variety of reasons for overeating or bingeing or purging. First, make an appointment with a doctor and a nutritionist experienced in eating disorders. They can run tests to see if hormones or chemical imbalances are contributing to your eating.

Successfully handling your compulsive eating means responding to the cause. The rest of this section focuses on responding to these causes.

CHAPTER 6

When Something Is Physically Wrong

Two years ago my husband became a compulsive eater. He was hungry all the time, and he never seemed to stay full for long. He was also cold much of the time, even on warm days. While other people would be driving down the highway with their windows open, we'd have our windows closed and the heater on.

My husband didn't seem overly stressed, and he wasn't gaining weight. We couldn't understand the source of the overeating.

Our family doctor finally discovered the reason for his overeating. He had a hyperactive thyroid gland. That means his thyroid was working too much. Destroying the thyroid that was overproducing hormone was the only cure. Once that happened, and my husband took the appropriate doses of synthetic thyroid hormone, his ravenous appetite disappeared.

The point of this story is that compulsive eating can result from biological causes that are completely separate from emotional causes. If you don't consider the biological possibilities first, you may prolong the time spent trying to fix the problem.

Does compulsive eating stem from one cause more than the other? Statistics are not easily available, but most people probably suffer more from emotional causes or unhealthy patterns of behavior than from biological causes. However, because biological problems do explain some compulsive eating, it's important to examine and rule out those causes first.

CHECK WITH THE EXPERTS

Your strategy for dealing with compulsive eating should first include a visit to your doctor. She'll check you for signs of hypoglycemia, diabetes, and thyroid disease. She'll test your blood, listen to your heart and lungs, and take a thorough medical history. She'll want to know any unusual symptoms you've been experiencing, how long you've had them, and any new circumstances that might account for the symptoms. It's best to arrive at the doctor's office equipped with as much information about yourself as you can provide. Don't assume that your only job is to get yourself to the appointment. A doctor can miss things without your active involvement.

If the doctor finds nothing physically wrong to account for your compulsive eating, your next stop should be the nutritionist. He or she will take another history to determine whether dietary deficiencies are contributing to your compulsive eating habits. Although all nutritionists are knowledgeable about dietary deficiencies, some have additional training in eating disorders. These are the best people to see for an assessment. Even if they specialize in working with people who purge, they are still aware of the difficulties that bingeing alone presents.

Some of the disorders that doctors and nutritionists may uncover include hypoglycemia, thyroid dysfunction, and diabetes. All three require monitoring by a physician; the latter two also require medication. You cannot self-treat diabetes and thyroid disease; these are life-threatening disorders. Diabetes can be managed by diet, oral medication, and insulin.

A person with an overactive thyroid will probably need to have his thyroid destroyed, either through surgery or by taking radioactive iodine, which kills the thyroid within six weeks. Once the thyroid has been destroyed, the person will need to take synthetic thyroid for the rest of his life, because the thyroid is vital to the human body. It controls metabolism: how fast we process food and how well we modulate our temperature. Once the appropriate amount of thyroid hormone is present in the body, the compulsive eating should stop.

Treatment for hypoglycemia is essentially the same for everyone, no matter what the specific cause is. The person with hypoglycemia should eat several small meals a day, consisting of complex carbohydrates (like potatoes or pasta), whole grains, and beans.

To help your pancreas, you should avoid sugar as much as possible, because sugar stimulates the production of insulin. Avoiding sugar means avoiding fruit juices that are high in sugar. Diets low in sugar won't stress the pancreas by calling on it too frequently to produce insulin. Eating intact food (like apples) is better than drinking apple juice, because cooking and mashing foods causes mineral and vitamin loss.

Your nutritionist can give you advice on healthy eating habits and help you decide if you need to take chromium or other supplements.

Carbohydrate and Sugar Cravings

Carbohydrate and sugar cravings can result from causes other than hypoglycemia. Low serotonin production can leave you craving carbohydrates. Serotonin is a brain chemical needed for mood stability, control of impulsivity, and appetite. Too little of it will cause depression, anger and irritability, sleep loss, and carbohydrate craving. That craving is the body's way of restoring its serotonin level, because the tryptophan in carbohydrates is the building block of serotonin. Chromium supplements will help increase the amounts of tryptophan reaching the brain.

No tests exist to determine how much serotonin a person produces, but doctors can get a good idea from the symptoms produced and a person's response to a group of antidepressant medications called selective serotonin reuptake inhibitors (SSRIs). If you have a low level of serotonin, you are likely to have other symptoms besides carbohydrate cravings—usually depression and irritability. Again, the solution is to choose a diet rich in complex carbohydrates, and see a nutritionist for specific advice about vitamin and mineral supplements.

Antidepressant Medications

A low serotonin level should respond to selective serotonin reuptake inhibitor (SSRI) medications, which are dispensed by a doctor. SSRIs are a form of antidepressant that specifically works to improve serotonin levels. Other antidepressants increase levels of both serotonin and norepinephrine, with the result that people get hungry and gain weight.

Serotonin is produced in neurons, which are the brain's

nerve cells, and is released into the synapses (the spaces between the neurons). Then the chemical is absorbed back into the releasing neuron to be used again. The longer serotonin lingers in the synapse, the greater the effect on mood instability, depression, and appetite control. Thus, serotonin reuptake inhibitors slow the reabsorption of serotonin into the neuron, causing it to linger in the synapse longer. Selective serotonin reuptake inhibitors include the drugs Prozac, Zoloft, Luvox, Paxil, and Effexor. These medications are very expensive prescriptions; you could pay between $60 and $160 for a month's prescription.

People who take other antidepressant medications may find they are hungry all the time or are simply putting on weight. The reason probably has to do with the brain chemicals that the specific antidepressants affect. Those that affect both norepinephrine and serotonin will cause more compulsive eating than the selective serotonin reuptake inhibitors that simply affect serotonin. That's because norepinephrine is the chemical that signals us that we're hungry. Serotonin signals us when we're full. Those antidepressants that target norepinephrine, such as the tricyclics, stimulate people's appetites. Asking your doctor to switch your antidepressant to a serotonin reuptake inhibitor may help control your compulsive eating. Sometimes one antidepressant is preferred over another for reasons unrelated to appetite, so it's not a good idea to substitute your friend's antidepressant for yours.

Sometimes tricyclic antidepressants have the opposite effect on appetite. As a rule, they stimulate appetite, but Gregory, a boy I know who takes Imipramine (an antidepressant), has been losing weight steadily. In his case, the medication alleviated his depression. Gregory had been an emotional eater who turned to food to deal with his sadness, and as he started to feel less depressed, he was not so interested in eating all the time. The antidepressant actually helped him regain control of his appetite.

Restored levels of serotonin seem to be responsible for managing compulsive behavior in general. People who take Prozac or Luvox often gain control over obsessive/compulsive symptoms, such as excessive hand washing and checking to see that doors are locked. Many doctors suspect a link between obsessive/compulsive behavior and compulsive eating.

If sugar cravings are a result of an untreated yeast infection, the underlying infection must first be treated. *Candida*, the medical term for yeast infections, is treated with an antifungal medication available in drug stores without a prescription. However, it's important to consult a doctor before taking any medication.

Food Sensitivities

If a doctor or nutritionist suspects that you have either a sensitivity or an allergy, he'll suggest that you eliminate all the "culprits" from your diet for a period of four weeks. This is called an elimination diet. If your symptoms disappear during the elimination diet, you probably have allergies or sensitivities to those foods you have eliminated.

To follow an elimination diet, you stop eating all the foods that contain the ingredients to which you're sensitive. That means you have to read the list of ingredients every time you shop for a product. Finding a product that doesn't contain sugar or corn syrup (another form of sugar) can be harder than you realize—so you have to look carefully!

Foods to which you're sensitive can be reintroduced in

small amounts into your diet once your body seems able to handle them. Foods to which you're actually allergic must be permanently eliminated from your diet.

Elimination diets work because you may gradually discover that you feel much better when not eating these particular foods. Later, when you reintroduce these foods a little at a time, you may experience headaches, depression, and fatigue. At that point, you're fully aware of the consequences of eating foods to which you're sensitive. Other people may find that they can build up a tolerance to the offending foods so that indulging in them won't cause a chain reaction of discomfort and cravings.

Some women become compulsive eaters in the week preceding their periods. This probably reflects a hormonal imbalance that can be helped by eating foods that will raise estrogen levels: milk products, eggs, and legumes. It's also important to maintain a sufficiently high magnesium level, not simply by taking vitamin and mineral supplements, but by keeping the minerals in proper balance. A nutritionist can advise you on how to keep proper balance, either through altering your diet or through vitamin/mineral supplements.

MANAGING ADDICTIONS

For people who appear addicted to sugar, treatment involves eliminating the foods the addict cannot handle, as well as involvement in a recovery support group such as Overeaters Anonymous. Groups like this help you cope with abstinence from the food you're addicted to and working through the emotional reasons for turning to food. These groups are usually free.

Many people believe alcoholics have a different chemistry from their nonalcoholic peers. Alcoholics seem predisposed to lose control over certain substances that don't affect nonalcoholics in the same way. Some say that alcoholics are born that way: they produce fewer endorphins (the body's natural pain-relieving chemicals), and the substances they abuse tend to restore their sense of well-being.

Food addicts appear to show the same type of behavior. They treat food the way an alcoholic treats alcohol. The more they eat sweet or starchy foods, the more they crave. Giving up sweets entirely is hard to do, which is why support groups are so helpful. All addictive behaviors have similar traits, so groups that recognize and try to deal with the overwhelming cravings that abstinent people still get are bound to be very helpful, no matter what the craving.

Biology doesn't explain all compulsive eating. If the doctor and nutritionist say there's nothing wrong with you physically, then you need to consider whether your overeating stems from emotional needs or from unhealthy learned patterns of behavior, or from both. That's the subject of the next chapter.

CHAPTER 7

Dealing with Feelings and Unhealthy Patterns of Behavior

Once you know your compulsive eating doesn't stem from a physical cause, or you've taken steps to correct the physical problem, you're ready to look at your emotional relationship to food. The emotional reasons for compulsive eating might not be easy to identify, so this is when you need to do some good detective work.

IDENTIFYING PATTERNS

A food diary is a good way to identify the circumstances in which you overeat or eat unhealthy things. There are two ways to keep a food diary. You can make a diary out of an ordinary notebook by writing down three headings:

WHAT I ATE, HOW MUCH I ATE, and WHAT FEEL-
ING OR SITUATION TRIGGERED THE EATING. You
must be diligent about writing down everything you eat;
it's usually the stuff you don't think is significant that
counts. If it's too scary to record everything you eat in a
day, make an effort to record as much as possible.

The other way to keep track of the food you eat, and
the situations that prompt you to overeat, is easier. You
simply draw circles in your notebook to represent how
much you ate at a time. Bigger circles represent bigger
meals, including your regular mealtimes. People who
snack a lot may have several smaller circles spread out
over their page. Write the times you ate in the circles. A
typical day may look like this:

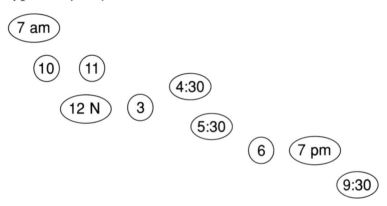

or like this, if you eat regular meals and then overeat at
night:

After a week or two of keeping a food diary (and it may not take that long to see your pattern), you'll be able to make connections between what and when you eat and how you're feeling. Once you've made that connection, you can decide how to handle the problem. Remember, the idea of keeping a food diary is not to make you feel worse by showing how much you eat. Instead, it is a positive tool that can show you how you're using food in an unhealthy way.

RECOGNIZING TRIGGERS

A food diary can show three things: how certain circumstances will trigger eating when you're not hungry; how certain feelings can trigger eating; and how ingrained habits can make you want to eat. Once you recognize the triggers, you can learn ways to avoid them. Avoiding them altogether is easier than ignoring the triggers once they're activated. For example, Julie realized that she couldn't walk past the bakery on her way home without wanting to go inside and buy a pastry. The problem was that she couldn't buy just one pastry; she would buy a dozen. Then, she'd feel guilty after she'd eaten a couple, but she couldn't bring herself to throw the rest away because she spent so much money on them. Since no one would be at home, she knew she'd eat them all herself; she couldn't stand to have them around.

If Julie doesn't walk past the bakery in the first place, she has no desire to buy any pastries. In her case, she curbed much of her afternoon snacking simply by taking another route home.

Avoiding triggers of association is called breaking behavioral chains. You may have gotten into the habit of eating around certain people or in certain situations. It has nothing to do with being hungry. You get used to eating pizza with friends on Friday night; you get used to eating your way through the store when you go grocery shopping; and you binge when you find open bags of cookies or candy bars in the cupboard. It may be easier to stave off a binge if you don't put yourself in the trigger situation.

If you always eat with certain friends, try a different activity. If your friends are not supportive of your change in eating habits, avoid these people, because they will most likely hurt your efforts. If you can't walk past stores without buying binge foods, avoid being near the stores. Ask someone else in your family to do the grocery shopping.

If you're the type of person who can manage her cravings just fine as long as the trigger foods aren't present, you must make the effort to avoid all trigger associations: certain foods, people, and situations.

DEALING WITH FEELINGS

The majority of emotional eaters binge to cover up their feelings. Some people binge when they're angry, some when they're depressed, and others when they're anxious. Use your diary to discover which feelings push you toward food. Then you may be able to learn a more appropriate way to handle that feeling.

If you eat when you're anxious, take a look at what kinds of situations make you anxious. Can you do anything about these situations to lessen your anxiety? It's usually the combination of feeling anxious and powerless to make any changes that sets people up to binge.

Conflict often makes people feel anxious, because most people view conflict as a negative event and want to be rid of it. Actually, conflict is neither good nor bad; it simply *is*. If a situation causes you discomfort, you need to meet it head on. Clarify the problem so that you can then work toward a solution. Some people are afraid to speak up to authority figures such as teachers. Then, believing the problem to be unsolvable, they may go home and eat. It is much healthier to meet with the teacher, discuss the problem, and decide together how to fix things.

If you can't immediately fix a problem, you can still find ways to relieve anxiety. Some people meditate each morning or in times of stress, such as right before a major test. You don't have to chant or repeat a mantra when you meditate; you simply try to empty your thoughts and clear your mind. Exhale slowly, concentrate on the sounds around you, and tune in to your own breathing. The mind can't hold onto two different feelings at once. You won't remain anxious if you can train yourself to calm down under stress.

Some people visualize calming situations when they're stressed. Some people remember a favorite TV episode, especially one that made them laugh. It's hard to remain anxious when you're laughing.

THE BENEFITS OF EXERCISE

Exercising helps some people work off their anxiety, and there may be a chemical reason behind this. Hard exercise releases endorphins into the bloodstream and brain. Endorphins are the body's natural pain relievers. They heighten your sense of well-being while decreasing your awareness of pain.

Exercising can be as simple as taking a brisk walk around the neighborhood. Don't think you have to commit yourself to a rigorous workout every day to manage your anxiety. Compulsive eating can lead to other forms of compulsive behavior, such as compulsive exercising. You don't want to trade one compulsion for another. However, walking, running, playing a hard game of racquetball, or shooting some hoops can be a good way to work off steam. And if it increases your endorphin production, that's an added bonus.

Finally, it's sometimes better to talk out your stress with friends than to go home and eat. You may feel better after sharing with others, even if the problem doesn't appear solvable. The act of sharing it with someone else decreases the anxiety. The less anxiety, the less need to binge and purge.

Trauma is the one situation that does not easily lend itself to self-help measures. If you eat to avoid dealing with feelings of anxiety or rage stirred up by trauma, you need to seek help from a professional.

DEALING WITH ANGER

Let's take a closer look at anger. Anger surfaces to protect us from feeling vulnerable. When you're feeling angry, it's usually because you're either frustrated by not getting something you wanted, fearful of losing something valuable, or hurt that you have already lost something valuable. That something of value can be another person, or it can be your self-esteem. The fear of "losing face" can make a lot of people angry.

Better than eating, which helps you avoid dealing with the primary emotions or the anger itself, you can find safe ways to examine the anger and to do something about it. You might start by writing down what is making you angry.

Chances are you won't know at first, so write whatever comes into your head. When you hit on what's making you angry, your gut level response will cue you. You'll probably feel a flash of recognition.

Next, try to figure out what the primary emotion is behind the anger. Are you really hurt about something or afraid you might have lost something?

Figuring out your anger and the primary emotion beneath it is only half the job. Next you have to decide how you'll deal with the problem.

Dealing with angry feelings can be as simple as:

1. Clarifying the problem and identifying the source of your anger.
2. Unmasking the primary emotion beneath the anger.
3. Dealing directly with the person or the situation making you angry.
4. Describing the problem behavior and explaining how it affects you.
5. Listening to the other side.
6. Working together toward a solution.

If you're too angry to think straight, grab a pen or sit at the computer and start writing. Exercise, or try meditation. Don't stew about what's making you angry. Think through the secondary emotion (anger) and look for the primary emotion. Decide on a course of action. Don't expect to get your way simply because you confronted the person with whom you're angry. He may see things differently. Working toward a solution means taking both of your needs into account. The idea is to change your habit of eating when angry to meeting problems head-on.

DEALING WITH BOREDOM

Some people eat out of loneliness, which may be hard to distinguish from boredom. Rather than eat, you could find ways to motivate herself. If you're truly lonely, you can take the initiative and join a club. You can volunteer at a library or in a nursing home. Some people feel more comfortable having a role that's either clearly defined or comes with a little authority. That way, they don't have to feel as if they're on the sidelines.

If it's boredom rather than loneliness that motivates you to eat, keep a list of things you can do when you're by yourself and bored. Keep your hands busy. If they're doing something, they're not free to reach for snacks.

If you're not sure whether you're feeling bored or lonely, you can do this simple exercise. Make a chart with these headings: SOMETHING REWARDING TO DO, SELF/OTHERS, HOW MUCH I WOULD ENJOY IT, and HOW MUCH I DID ENJOY IT. Then fill in the categories. Write down a couple of things you could do that you know would be enjoyable. Make one of them a solitary activity, and one an activity done with another person. Estimate how much you would enjoy this activity, using a scale of 0 (not enjoying it at all) to 100 (having the time of your life). After you've done this activity, rate how much you really enjoyed each activity. Do this exercise for several activities; you may discover that you enjoy the solitary activities as much as the ones you do with other people. Therefore, it's not so much that you're lonely, because you can clearly have a good time when you're alone. It's probably more likely that you're bored, having nothing in particular to do.

If you're feeling lonely because you miss someone,

write him or her a letter. Even if you don't know this person's whereabouts, you can still write down your feelings.

DEALING WITH NEGATIVE THINKING

If you eat when you're depressed, you may not realize that you can do something more positive about your depression. I encourage my depressed clients to take a good look at the unhappy events in their lives and figure out what they're telling themselves about these events. Bad events don't always get people down; it's what people tell themselves the bad events mean.

Once you can turn your negative thoughts into more realistic appraisals of the upsetting event, you should find yourself feeling less depressed. You will discover that it's not the event that disturbs you as much as what you tell yourself the event means. If you can change your thinking, you will feel less depressed.

Keep this chart handy for those moments you're hit with negative thoughts. Writing them down helps you see how unrealistic most of them can be.

UPSETTING EVENT	NEGATIVE THOUGHTS	MORE REALISTIC APPRAISAL

For example, one person's upsetting event might be: *Mom is drinking again.* Her negative thoughts might be: *I'll have to manage the household now and won't have time for basketball. Then my coach will throw me off the team, and I'll never get to play for any other team. I'll lose my skills and won't get a basketball scholarship to college, so I'll probably never get to go to college.*

These negative thoughts sound dramatic, but that's often what happens when we let our thoughts run away with us. We just don't usually put them down on paper, so we don't realize how exaggerated they sound.

Next, decide what's wrong with these thoughts, or what you can do to keep these thoughts from actually happening. In this example, the girl could have realized that her coach wouldn't throw her off the team if she approached him with the problem. Or even if he had let her go, she still was a good enough player that someone else might pick her up. In the worst case, she might not be playing basketball, and might lose some of her skills, but that doesn't mean she'd never get to college. There are other types of scholarships, in addition to grants and loans. The upsetting event—her mom's drinking—wasn't causing her to feel so out of control. Her mistaken beliefs were causing her to feel out of control. If she realistically confronted her fears, she'd feel more in control.

DEALING WITH EMOTION

For some people, any strong emotion triggers compulsive eating. If you're one of them, ask yourself why you suddenly feel like eating. If you overeat when you're happy, is it because you're afraid your good feelings won't last? Is it because you don't think you deserve to be happy? These feelings will come out if you begin to deal with them through self-help measures.

First, if you have trouble making positive changes in your life, you may find that it's your family that's working to keep you from changing. Take the following TRUE/FALSE test to see if your family tends to sabotage your plans.

1. My family members don't have control over their own eating habits. T/F
2. Family members are not actively involved with people outside the family or in nonfood activities. T/F
3. Family members are not supportive when I want to do things outside the home or without them. T/F
4. Family members think my weight and eating habits are not significant problems. T/F

The more TRUES you answered, the more likely your family resists your making some healthy changes. If that's the case, you'll want to find a better support system. Sometimes people need more help than their families can give.

A food diary is one self-help measure that pinpoints what feelings and situations prompt you to binge. Most likely, you'll find that you binge when you feel that you have no control over a certain situation. If that's the case, you can then learn how to delay your binges.

Again, it will help to write down the upsetting event. Then record your negative thoughts about that event. You have to be able to figure out the upsetting events and realize what negative thoughts you're having. Then, the solution lies in attacking the negative thoughts, because the thoughts are the problem, more than the event. You can always change your thoughts, even if you can't necessarily change the event.

If you've done this exercise, but still feel a need to eat, then it's okay for now. Recognizing the triggers of your binges is a big step in the right direction, even if you are not yet able to refrain from overeating, or bingeing and purging.

As you become more aware of your triggers, try to avoid

them altogether. That's usually easier than trying to deal with them before you have the resources to do so.

Another measure will aid you in recognizing the signs of being full. You can learn to do three things:

1. Eat more slowly. Eating should not be a race.
2. Chew your food thoroughly. Chewing everything at least twenty times will force you to slow down. Chewing activates the stomach juices used to digest food. As you start to chew, the fifteen minutes needed to signal the brain that the stomach is full begin ticking away.
3. Stop eating when you sense that you're no longer hungry. That means leaving some food on your plate if you sense that you're full before you've eaten everything. If you force yourself to eat until you're stuffed, you lose the ability to sense that physical discomfort, or you grow accustomed to that discomfort. If you leave food on your plate, you'll eventually learn to moderate your helpings, because you'll know you won't comfortably be able to eat more than that.

Since you might not be aware of the signs of hunger, it might help to draw yourself a chart that looks something like this:

Very hungry   Stuffed

Whenever you're tempted to eat something, draw a line on this graph indicating how you feel right then and there. What you want to do is reach a middle point, being neither too hungry nor stuffed. You'll want to keep from hitting that "very hungry" point, and learn to stop eating before you reach the "stuffed" point.

Each time you draw your hunger graph and decide not to eat unless you're really hungry (falling left of center), you remind yourself that eating and being physically hungry go together. Each time you stop eating because you're full, you teach yourself not to overindulge. After a while, you won't need to keep the chart, because you'll be able to feel when you're hungry or full.

If you eat to reward yourself, find other ways besides food to treat yourself. Take a nice bubble bath; call a friend long distance; buy an inexpensive book you've been wanting. The idea here is to break the connection between food and a reward.

If your family celebrates with food, introduce other activities in its place. Maybe they celebrate with food because that's what they've always done. Give them some other options; for example, make games a part of your activities.

Finally, if you nibble a lot during the day, keep your hands busy. Reflect on your hunger chart; don't eat if you're not really hungry. If you like to sample food while you cook and can't seem to refrain, eat a sour pickle first. The taste will turn you off from eating something sweet. If you don't have any sour pickles handy, go brush your teeth. Clean, fresh teeth and the minty taste of toothpaste may turn you off from eating too.

Most important of all, don't be hard on yourself. Do the best you can to make sense of your eating habits, and if you slip up, consider yourself human and go on from there. If you're an emotional eater, you'll be tempted to soothe yourself with food once you slip up, and then you'll condemn yourself. Recognize this tendency in yourself, and your slips will be fewer. You learn from your mistakes.

CHAPTER 8

Getting
Professional Help

I f you are hesitant to go to a professional, please remember that many people eat compulsively because of unresolved emotional conflicts. Self-help books can pinpoint the problems for you, but sometimes you need to sit down and talk those problems out.

It takes a great deal of courage to seek help. Going to a therapist or counselor does not mean you're "crazy," nor does it mean that you are "took weak" to handle your problems yourself. These attitudes are false. Therapy helps you live a good life under very trying circumstances.

People who eat compulsively may benefit from therapy especially because they may also may demonstrate other forms of compulsive behavior. Compulsive eaters may also be compulsive shoppers, drinkers, or exercisers. Obsessive/compulsive traits respond well to a therapy regimen of medication (usually SSRIs) and behavioral approaches. The medication helps curb the compulsive behavior; the behavioral strategies help the individual make positive changes in the way she's dealt with compulsions in the past. Sometimes group treatment for compulsive behavior is the most helpful of all, because other individuals with similar compulsions can share their insights and strategies.

Bingeing and purging can also stem from sexual abuse and early trauma. Both require therapy to help the individual recover and move on in her life. When people have been abused, they sometimes turn to compulsive eating to comfort them. Food also serves as the focus of their days, temporarily enabling them to avoid thinking about the source of their pain. Food becomes a stand-in for their feelings about the abuse they suffered.

Treatment for chronic trauma, such as sexual abuse, first involves establishing safety—coping with strong feelings, learning to obtain support from at least one person, learning when to trust and when not to trust others, and trusting and taking care of the self. Once basic safety needs are met, it is possible to explore past trauma while monitoring and stabilizing the compulsive eating. The victim needs to learn that he was not to blame for the abuse, to grieve his losses (which include the loss of innocence), and to move on with his life.

TYPES OF THERAPISTS

When you realize that your compulsive eating is caused by emotional conflicts, you may consider professional counseling. But who is the best person to see?

An eating disorder program or therapist who specializes in eating disorders is best, because these professionals have extensive training and experience in treating these conditions. You can check with hospitals in your area to learn if they have an eating disorder program or can recommend therapists who specialize in treating eating disorders. Sometimes these are listed in the Yellow Pages of your phone book.

Your second choice is to find a qualified professional who takes clients with compulsive eating patterns of behavior. But which type of professional is best?

Different professionals are good for different reasons. A psychiatrist is a doctor with a medical degree who is licensed to prescribe medication. If your compulsive eating stems from a chemical imbalance or physical disorder, he or she is the only one who can order medicine for your condition. A psychiatrist also is the most expensive person to consult. Most people can't afford weekly visits to a psychiatrist unless their health insurance covers this type of care.

Primary care doctors may sometimes prescribe medication for compulsive overeating, but if they suspect another type of disorder, such as an endocrine disorder, they'll usually refer the individual to another doctor, such as an endocrinologist, for a more elaborate workup.

Psychologists are professionals who have a Ph.D. or Psy.D. in clinical psychology, or a Ph.D. or Ed.D. in counseling psychology. Although some psychologists have a master's degree in psychology, in the future, most will be required to have a doctorate. The more credentials the therapist has, the more costly the appointment as a rule.

Clinical social workers are therapists with either a doctorate in social work or a Master of Social Work degree. Some people, called licensed professional counselors, do the same work as clinical social workers, but have graduate degrees in related mental health fields.

Clinical psychiatric nurses are therapists with a master's degree in nursing. They can be particularly helpful in the treatment of eating disorders because, as nurses, they are well aware of the physical consequences of compulsive eating (and purging).

QUALITIES TO CONSIDER

Three factors come into play when considering which type of professional you will choose.

1. Choose a professional who is licensed. Anyone in private practice or accepting third-party reimbursement (payment from insurance companies) will be licensed as a rule. Licensure means that the person has passed the required courses of instruction, has been supervised for the required number of hours, and has passed a state or national exam.

2. Choose a therapist whose style fits with your personality. That doesn't mean you have to like everything your therapist does. Looking at problems is hard work, and most people resist it at some point. A therapist's job is to explore your situation and keep you focused on the task at hand. You won't always like that, and it's not meant to be fun. However, some therapists fit better with certain clients than others. It's more a matter of personality than how qualified they are.

3. A good therapist will respect boundaries. Therapy is a working relationship. If your therapist suggests anything else, switch therapists or consult another therapist about the appropriateness of the treatment.

OTHER COUNSELORS

Other counselors exist to help people with their problems, but they are better suited to different problems. For example, school counselors are a logical choice for school-related difficulties. Certified alcohol and drug counselors are good choices for people who have substance abuse problems in addition to problems with compulsive eating. Ministers are helpful to those people whose difficulties are spiritual.

As a rule, though, people with eating disorders (bingeing and purging or compulsive eating) respond best to trained professionals who have experience treating eating disorders. It's true that some people need their depression treated before they can make progress on their compulsive eating, but it's much more difficult to get rid of one problem without addressing the other. Compulsive eating still needs to be addressed and managed even if the underlying depression must be taken care of first. A therapist who is familiar with eating disorders or compulsive behavior may be more useful than the therapist who only treats depression.

SPECIFIC TREATMENT FOR BULIMICS

Bulimics, or people who binge and purge, are seriously hurting their bodies. Hospitalization is usually necessary to repair physical damage and to get the compulsive eating under control. Depending on how seriously ill she is, a person who binges and purges will either go to a regular hospital or to an inpatient eating disorder program. Doctors and nurses at a regular hospital are equipped only to manage the physical manifestations of bingeing and purging. They can correct dehydration and monitor cardiac problems; they can medicate gastrointestinal problems; but they're not always trained to deal with the psychological issues that prompt the bingeing and purging behavior. That's why most patients must enter an eating disorder program at some point.

A structured program includes individual therapy, group therapy, and family therapy. Some doctors will prescribe medication if they think the patient has a chemical imbalance that is partly responsible for the bingeing behavior. Staff also monitor the patient's eating and educate him about the damage he's doing to his body.

Group therapy appears to be the most effective type of therapy for people with serious eating disorders because patients can learn just as much from their peers as from the therapist. The issues for patients who binge and purge are rarely about food. Focusing on food (how much the individual eats, how much she vomits, how many laxatives she uses or refrains from using) keeps the spotlight off the other issues in the person's life. Other bulimics may wonder about the conflicts the individual is avoiding; they may wonder how that person handles her anger.

Bulimics do not necessarily have an excessively low body weight. They often look like average teenagers, neither overweight, nor skin and bones. Their purging offsets their binges. They're not usually trying to attain a perfect body. For them, the issue seems to be not knowing how to handle being "out of control."

Therapists, whether in an inpatient or outpatient setting, teach bulimics ways to feel more in control. A food diary may pinpoint the feelings or situation that bring on a binge, making it easier to determine how the bulimic needs to deal with the stress. Bulimics who purge have to learn two things: how to eat regular amounts of food, and how to refrain from purging afterward.

Bulimia almost always relates to things happening in the family. For this reason, family therapy is important in treatment. The idea is not to assign blame; rather, it's to focus on the communication patterns in the family and to learn what situations are troubling the patient. Often the person who binges and purges is unknowingly sacrificing herself so that other troubling aspects of the family go unnoticed. For example, therapists sometimes discover that a child acts out when the parents are having marital problems. The child unwittingly acts out so that her parents will focus their joint attention on her difficulties and forget that they're angry with each other and contemplating divorce.

Sometimes, therapists discover that a girl wants to grow up, but the parents are afraid to let her. Because they try to control her, the parents are creating a climate the child can rebel against. At the same time, the child feels overcontrolled by her parents and out of control with her feelings. The child can't stop eating, but tries to minimize the damage by controlling what stays in her body.

Families are not always interested in being included in treatment. Unfortunately, if they don't want to accept treatment, they convey the message that the "problem" has nothing to do with them.

SUPPORT GROUPS

Many support groups are formulated on twelve-step programs and, like Alcoholics Anonymous and Al-Anon, are highly successful in helping people manage their compulsive behavior. Some people can find help for their compulsions through therapy, but still have trouble fully reining them in. They may know why they focus on food, but they're ineffective in changing their habits.

Aretha was both severely depressed and a compulsive eater. She got into therapy and worked hard to resolve her feelings of emptiness and rage, stemming from early physical and sexual abuse at the hands of her stepfather and an elderly baby-sitter. While Aretha made a lot of progress in therapy, she still couldn't seem to stop overeating. In fact, she often compulsively stole food from the local grocery store.

She minimized what she did. "The lines were too long at the check-out, so I just walked out with the stuff." Or, "I didn't have enough money for the food right then, and I figured I could pay it back later when I got my check."

Exploring Aretha's compulsive stealing as well as her compulsive eating had little effect on her behavior. What eventually helped her was joining Overeaters Anonymous, where she found many people like herself. "Other people steal food, too," she marveled. "It's part of our addictive cycle."

Aretha found a sponsor, and called her when she found herself headed out the door to the grocery store. "I just couldn't control the behavior by myself," she said. "Therapy gave me the tools to examine my past and what I was doing, but Overeaters Anonymous gave me the support to actually resist the behavior."

People who determine that their compulsive eating is a form of addictive behavior will benefit from groups like Overeaters Anonymous (OA). These support groups are run by people with similar addictions. They offer emotional support, acceptance and understanding, and a strategy for coping with an addiction. They recognize that certain occasions pose more of a problem than others for the food addict, and they offer advice for how to get through these occasions.

Sometimes, groups like OA are all the support a person needs to change her behavior. Other times, OA is an additional treatment to therapy; both are helpful in managing aspects of compulsive eating.

There is no minimum age for joining Overeaters Anonymous. Anyone who feels that he or she has trouble controlling his or her behavior around food can join.

If you can't find an Overeaters Anonymous group in your area (they're usually listed in the phone book), you can write to the address listed in the "Where to Go for Help" section at the end of this book for the name and number of the closest group.

DIFFERENCE BETWEEN OA AND DIET GROUPS

Some people join diet groups to gain control over their compulsive eating. If dieting were the answer, these support groups would be more helpful. However, the problem is not that you weigh too much. People who binge and purge don't necessarily need to lose weight; they are probably of average size. When you join a weight-loss group, the focus is on losing weight, and you are supported in your efforts to control your intake and shed "unwanted" pounds.

Overeaters Anonymous is a better alternative, for it focuses on helping you recover physically and emotionally from compulsive overeating. The focus is on your eating patterns instead of on your weight. In order to cope, you may need to rely on a spiritual power as well, and many groups will encourage that aspect of your recovery.

CHAPTER 9

When a Friend Is a Compulsive Eater

There are things you can do (and not do) to help and support a friend who is dealing with an eating disorder.

1. Never nag your friend about her weight or her compulsive eating. Nagging doesn't get anyone to change her behavior, but it does lead to resentment. Resentment often leads to acting out. If she brings the subject up, all you really need to do is listen.

2. Don't socialize with food all the time. Pick other activities to do with your friend. If you introduce other activities, you'll be helping to break out of this pattern. Just try not to make a big deal out of it.

3. Remain nonjudgmental, even if your friend decides he doesn't want to get control of his compulsive eating. If you judge him, you'll find him lacking, and he will sense this. Sensing your disapproval, he may feel bad about himself and find it even harder to get control of his

behavior. Or he may be angry that he feels he has to live up to your expectations.

4. Never offer your friend advice unless he asks for it. If he's really asking for your advice, he will say, "What do you think . . ."

Even then, be careful what you say. If you jump in too quickly with a solution, you may find he's changed his mind in the meantime and doesn't want advice anymore.

If he *does* ask you for advice, describe how you see the problem without being judgmental. And be careful not to play therapist. Simply tell him what you see. You can say, "I think you lose control around food and eat things that aren't always healthy."

Don't overwhelm him with too may observations or too dire a revelation, like "You know, I think you could probably lose 100 pounds and still be overweight." If you frustrate him before he even gets started, he won't have the desire to follow through.

5. If your friend decides she wants to join a support group, but is afraid to go alone that first time, offer to go with her. Chance are she'll meet other people like herself and won't need you to keep going with her. But you'll be helping her to get to that first meeting if you offer to go, too. But don't suggest the meeting if she hasn't decided that it is right for her.

6. Don't make a big deal out of your own weight, especially if it's more normal than hers. Don't talk endlessly about dieting.

WHEN IT'S IMPORTANT TO ACT

Bingeing and purging is a different story because your friend's health is being seriously compromised.

Sheila knew her friend Roxanne was throwing up

after eating in order to lose weight for the prom. She'd heard Roxanne in the bathroom throwing up after eating some chips one night when she stayed over at Sheila's house.

Sheila didn't know what to say or do. Should she tell Roxanne's mother or should she leave well enough alone? She decided to wait and see if this behavior continued.

A week later, the girls went out to eat pizza. When Roxanne excused herself after eating to go to the bathroom, Sheila sneaked into the bathroom after her. She heard Roxanne throwing up again. When Roxanne came out of the stall to wash her face, Sheila was standing there at the sink.

"Roxanne, you're bulimic, aren't you? How long have you been doing this?"

Startled, Roxanne put her hands over her face. "Don't tell anyone. It was only this one time."

"No, it isn't," Sheila said. "I heard you throwing up over at my house the other night."

"I only do it once in a while," Roxanne pleaded. "I'm not bulimic."

"You need to get some help," Sheila said, but she really didn't know what kind of help Roxanne needed.

"I'm just doing this to help lose some weight; I'm really okay."

Sheila walked out as a couple of other people came into the bathroom. She really thought she should do something, but she didn't want to betray her friend.

She avoided Roxanne for the next couple of weeks, but when Roxanne fainted during gym class, Sheila knew she had to do more than just watch her friend get more and more sick.

Sheila went to her gym teacher and said, "I think you should know that Roxanne is throwing up after she eats.

She's been doing this for several weeks that I know of. She won't get help."

The gym teacher frowned at Sheila. "Why didn't you tell somebody before this?" she said.

Sheila looked at the floor. "She told me not to tell."

"Bulimia is a life-threatening condition," the teacher said.

"But I wasn't sure she had that,' Sheila said.

The gym teacher saw how concerned Sheila was. "I guess you thought a friend didn't tell on a friend," she said. "In some cases, though, that's the best thing a friend can do."

When people have life-threatening conditions, such as bulimia or diabetes, they are severely ill. They often lose their judgment and don't realize how dangerous their situation has become. You may have to act in their behalf.

People with life-threatening conditions need medical treatment and counseling. Getting them to a doctor is the first order of business. Being a teenager, you're not necessarily in a position to take a friend in for medical treatment. You'll need to get her parents to take her. You can help by making your friend aware of the seriousness of her problem and advising her parents or a teacher so that they can do something for her.

Since bulimics fear changing their habits, your friend will probably resent your stepping in. You may want to *suggest* treatment first and let her make the decision to get it.

However, since many bulimics are unwilling to get help, you may have to take more action. If your friend won't get help on her own, you need to notify an adult who can intervene on her behalf. Your friend may feel you have betrayed her. However, if you fail to act when you know she is doing something harmful, then you will really be betraying the friendship.

Under no circumstances should you "play therapist" with your friend. (Even professional therapists don't counsel their friends.) That's because you're so involved with the person that you can't be objective about her condition. You also don't have the experience or training that a professional does. You can listen to your friend's problems, and you can empathize with her, but you can't make her well by keeping her self-destructive behavior a secret.

If your friend is a compulsive eater whose health is compromised by her overeating, you have to get through to her that it's her health that concerns you, not her appearance. You want to convey concern, not judgment. Ultimately, each person has to make up her own mind about getting control over compulsive eating. If you continually have to monitor it for her, she's not ready to make changes. It's only when people are interested in changing that they'll pick up a book like this. That's a start.

Your job is to stand along the sidelines and support your friend's efforts. If she slips up, don't lecture. Keep supporting. Let her know you are there if she needs you.

Appendix:
Eating Healthy

These are recommended servings of food to eat for maintaining good health. While each person's needs are different—it's important for you to find a balance you feel comfortable with—these are good guidelines to keep in mind.

The number of portions listed below include those that are appropriate for both teens and adults.

Food Group	Foods in This Group, and Serving Size	Number of Servings
Milk	1 cup milk; 1 cup plain yogurt; 1½ oz cheese; 2 cups cottage cheese; 1¾ cup ice cream or ice milk	Teens: 4 Adults: 2
Meat	2–3 oz cooked lean meat, poultry, or fish; 2 eggs; 1–1½ cup dried peas or beans; ½–1 cup nuts and seeds; 4 Tbsp peanut butter	Teens: 2 Adults: 2

Fruits	$\frac{1}{2}$ cup juice; $\frac{1}{2}$ cup fruit (canned, cooked); 1 cup fruit (raw); $\frac{1}{2}$ grapefruit or cantaloupe	Teens: 4 Adults: 4
Vegetables	$\frac{1}{2}$ cup juice; $\frac{1}{2}$ cup vegetable (canned, cooked); 1 cup vegetable (raw)	Teens: 4 Adults: 4
Grains	1 slice bread; 1 cup dry cereal; $\frac{1}{2}$ cup hot cereal or grits; $\frac{1}{2}$ cup rice; $\frac{1}{2}$ cup pasta	Teens: 4 Adults: 4
Fats, Sweets, Alcohol	1 tsp margarine or butter; 1 tsp sugar; 1 Tbsp mayonnaise; salad dressing; 1 Tbsp jelly; 1 cup soft drink	Use Sparingly

Where to Go for Help

HOT LINES

Bulimia Anorexia Self-Help
(800) BASH-STL

National Food Addiction Hot Line
(800) USA-0088

Overeaters Anonymous
(800) 743-8703

You can also look up local agencies in the Yellow Pages of your phone book. Look under:

Drug Abuse and Addiction Information and Treatment
Eating Disorders Information and Treatment
Mental Health—Centers and Counselors
Marriage and Family Counselors

INFORMATION

For information on weight loss groups or counselors, see Weight Control Services in the Yellow Pages.

National Eating Disorders Organization
6655 South Yale Avenue
Tulsa, OK 74136
(918) 481-4044

Overeaters Anonymous
P.O. Box 44020
Rio Rancho, NM 87174
(505) 891-2664

WEB SITES

Overeaters Anonymous
http://www.overeatersanonymous.org/

Online Psychological Services
http://www.onlinepsych.com/treat/mh.htm/

Psychology Self-Help Resources on the Internet
http://www.gasou.edu/psychweb/resource/selfhelp.htm/

Glossary

antidepressants   medications used to elevate a person's mood

ambivalence   a feeling of conflicting emotions about something, such as love and hate

anorexia   also called anorexia nervosa; a psychological condition in which a person is obsessed with weight loss and starves herself or himself

anorexic   a person with anorexia

bulimia   a continuous and seemingly inexplicable hunger

carbohydrate   a natural element of foods that supplies energy to the body

chromium   a mineral needed for normal body function

depression   an emotional condition often characterized by feelings of hopelessness, sadness, and inadequacy

diarrhea   excessive and very loose bowel movements, usually with a feeling of urgency; diarrhea can be a symptom of many different problems

diabetes   a disorder in which insulin production is reduced, resulting in increased sugar in the blood.

dopamine   a chemical in the brain essential to normal brain activity

endorphins   elements of the body chemistry that act as natural pain relievers

esophagus   the tube through which food passes from the mouth to the stomach

fast   a period of not eating ("breakfast" is breaking the fast of the night)

glucose   sugar that is used by the body for fuel

hypoglycemia   a physical condition in which the bloodstream contains a very low level of sugar

insulin   a hormone that helps the body use sugar and other carbohydrates

laxative   a medication that induces bowel movements

obesity   a condition of being 30 percent or more over one's ideal body weight

neurons   the cells that make up the nervous system in the body

neurotransmitters   chemicals that transmit nerve impulses between nerve cells

norepinephrine   a chemical in the body that transmits nerve impulses

pancreas   the organ in the body that secretes digestive juices and produces insulin

physiological   having to do with normal body functioning

potassium   a mineral essential to normal body functioning

serotonin   a chemical in the brain; its presence is considered to affect mood and appetite

tryptophan   an amino acid, produced naturally during digestion

For Further Reading

Appleton, Nancy. *Lick the Sugar Habit*. Garden City Park, NY: Avery Publishing Group, Inc., 1988.

Arensen, Gloria. *A Substance Called Food*. New York: McGraw-Hill, Inc., 1989.

Billigmeier, Shirley. *Inner Eating*. Nashville: Thomas Nelson Pub., 1991.

Fuchs, Nan Kathryn. *Overcoming Overeating*. Los Angeles: Lowell House, 1989.

Kamen, Betty. *The Chromium Connection*. Novato, CA: Nutrition Encounter, Inc., rev. ed., 1994.

Katz, Alice. *Eating Without Guilt*. North Vancouver, BC: International Self-Counsel Press Ltd., 1991.

LeBlanc, Donna. *What's Eating You*. Deerfield Beach, FL: Health Communications, Inc., 1990.

Maloney, Michael, and Krantz, Rachel. *Straight Talk About Eating Disorders*. New York: Facts on File, 1991.

Moe, Barbara. *Coping with Eating Disorders*, rev. ed. New York: Rosen Publishing Group, 1995.

——*Feeding the Hungry Heart*. New York: A Plume Book, 1993.

——*When Food Is Love*. New York: A Dutton Book, 1991.

Sheppard, Kay. *Food Addiction*. Deerfield Beach, FL: Health Communications, Inc., 1993.

Index

A
abuse
 as a cause for compulsive
  eating, 32–33
 treatment for, 67
addict, 25
addiction, managing, 52
anger
 as a cause for compulsive
  eating, 2, 31
 dealing with, 58–59
antidepressants
 types of, 49–50
anxiety
 and bingeing, 11
 and hypoglycemia, 17
 as a cause of compulsive
  eating, 31
 dealing with, 56–58

B
bingeing and purging
 and bulimia, 10
 and chemical imbalance, 26
 and sexual abuse, 32, 33, 67
 definition of, 7–11
 physical consequences of,
  15–16, 18
boredom
 as a cause for compulsive
  eating, 1, 31

dealing with, 60–61
bulimia
 and bingeing and purging,
  10, 33
 and sexual abuse, 33
 helping a friend with, 77–81
 treatment for, 71–73, 79–80

C
chemical imbalance, 26, 43
cleaning one's plate, 14, 35
compulsive behavior
 definition of, 6, 27
 treatment for, 50, 67
compulsive eating
 biological causes of
  identifying, 22–26, 45
  treating, 46–52
 definition of, 6
 emotional causes of
  dealing with, 56–66
  identifying, 1–3, 12, 14,
   26, 30–39, 53–56
 helping a friend, 76–80
 physical consequences,
  15–19
 social consequences, 19, 20
 types, 3–4, 6–14
compulsive overeating, 12–14
conflict
 dealing with, 56–57